OVERCOMING ADVERSITY:
SHARING THE AMERICAN DREAM

CHARLES BARKLEY

D1523623

MASON CREST PUBLISHERS
PHILADELPHIA

OVERCOMING ADVERSITY:
SHARING THE AMERICAN DREAM

OVERCOMING ADVERSITY:
SHARING THE AMERICAN DREAM

CHARLES BARKLEY

JAMIE FEDORKO

MASON CREST PUBLISHERS
PHILADELPHIA

ABOUT CROSS-CURRENTS

When you see this logo, turn to the Cross-Currents section at the back of the book. The Cross-Currents features explore connections between people, places, events, and ideas.

Produced by OTTN Publishing, Stockton, New Jersey

Mason Crest Publishers
370 Reed Road
Broomall, PA 19008
www.masoncrest.com

First printing

1 3 5 7 9 8 6 4 2

Library of Congress Cataloging-in-Publication Data

Fedorko, Jamie.
  Charles Barkley / Jamie Fedorko.
      p. cm. — (Sharing the American dream : overcoming adversity)
  Includes bibliographical references.
  ISBN 978-1-4222-0576-1 (hardcover) — ISBN 978-1-4222-0737-6 (pbk.)
 1. Barkley, Charles, 1963—Juvenile literature. 2. Basketball players—United States—
Biography—Juvenile literature. I. Title.
  GV884.B28F43 2008
  796.323092—dc22
  [B]
                                   2008028902

OVERCOMING ADVERSITY:
SHARING THE AMERICAN DREAM

TABLE OF CONTENTS

CHAPTER ONE

LIVING BIG

In the history of the National Basketball Association, only five players have amassed at least 20,000 points, 10,000 rebounds, and 4,000 assists: Wilt Chamberlain, Kareem Abdul-Jabbar, Kevin Garnett, Karl Malone, and Charles Barkley. As the statistics indicate, all were dominant players. In one respect, however, Charles Barkley stands out among this elite group. Chamberlain and Abdul-Jabbar both topped 7 feet tall, Garnett stands 6'11", and Malone played at 6'9". When he entered the NBA, Charles announced his height as 6'6". Sportswriters were skeptical, and Charles later admitted that he was actually a little under 6'5". In the NBA, that is the size of a big guard or a small forward. Yet, battling against much taller players, Charles established himself as one of the game's best power forwards, pulling down 12,546 rebounds during his 16-year career.

A Singular Star

Arguably, Charles Barkley redefined the position of power forward. Before him, teams relied on their power forwards mostly to rebound and block shots. Charles did both these things, of course, but he did much more. He was an offensive powerhouse. He had tantalizing one-on-one moves, his ball-handling skills

With his excellent ball-handling skills, his great quickness, and his extraordinary knack for rebounding, Charles Barkley helped redefine the position of power forward.

were outstanding for a power forward, and he was an excellent passer. He was a great jumper, with a vertical leap measured at more than 37 inches. He was too quick to be defended by most big men and too strong to be covered by most guards and small forwards. He also played relentless defense.

"He plays everything; he plays basketball," observed NBA legend and analyst Bill Walton. "There is nobody who does what Barkley does. He's a dominant rebounder, a dominant defensive player, a three-point shooter, a dribbler, a playmaker."

Walton's assessment is hardly an exaggeration. A brief look at Charles Barkley's career bears out his undeniable achievements on the court. Charles was an 11-time NBA All-Star, and in 1991 he was selected the All-Star Game's Most Valuable Player (MVP). Five times during his career, sportswriters and broadcasters voted him to the All-NBA First Team—meaning that Charles was considered one of the two best forwards in the league those years. In 1993, Charles won the Maurice Podoloff Trophy as the NBA's MVP for the 1992–93 season. He took home gold medals at the 1992 and 1996 Olympic Games. And in 1996, when the NBA announced the 50 greatest players of all time to mark the league's 50th year in existence, Charles Barkley was on that list.

READ MORE

Turn to page 44 to learn about the NBA's list of its 50 greatest players of all time.

Controversies and Contradictions

There is much more to Charles Barkley's story than basketball, however. During his playing days, Charles was almost as well known for what he did and said off the court as for his game-time heroics. Charles seemed to attract trouble. He was involved in numerous brawls in bars and nightclubs, and he was arrested a handful of times in connection with those incidents. Frequently, Charles also raised eyebrows with his words. Professional athletes are typically very cautious about what they say publicly. They tend to stick to sports or relatively innocuous subjects. Even then their utterances—much to the frustration of sportswriters— can be painfully trite. Not Charles Barkley. Charles never shied away from expressing his views, even on controversial subjects such as race and politics. And he wasn't bland, but direct, colorful, and frequently outrageous. Sometimes what Charles said was hilarious; other times, his words offended many people. But his outspokenness always attracted attention. That is one reason why, following Charles's retirement from pro basketball in 2000, TNT hired him as an analyst for its *Inside the NBA* show.

When his playing days were over, Charles Barkley easily stepped into the role of sports broadcaster. His infectious humor and blunt, often outrageous observations captivated viewers.

Behind the microphone, Charles found new fans—and helped the show win an Emmy Award—with his candor and his humor. Yet trouble and controversy continued to follow him. He ran up large gambling debts. He also racked up another arrest, for suspicion of driving under the influence of alcohol.

It might be tempting to dismiss Charles Barkley as another big-mouthed, bad-behaving, immature superstar. But that description hardly captures the complexity of the man. From the first years of his pro career, in Philadelphia, Charles gained a reputation for being approachable and down-to-earth. Off the court, he didn't act like a star. He also displayed—and continues

Charles spreads some smiles at Baystate Medical Center in Springfield, Massachusetts, September 8, 2006. From his first years in the NBA, he has been extraordinarily generous with his time and money.

to display—great generosity. In 2005, for example, Charles donated a million dollars to help victims of Hurricane Katrina. Two years earlier, he had been invited to speak at a conference on health issues affecting minorities at the University of Alabama at Birmingham. He not only accepted the invitation to speak, but also donated a large amount of money to launch the Charles Barkley Health Disparities Fund. The fund's goal is to improve access to health care for underserved minority communities in Alabama.

"Basketball is really important and significant in my life," Charles Barkley said in 2006, after being elected to the Naismith Memorial Basketball Hall of Fame, "but it's the least important thing. I'm supposed to do great things with my fame."

Some of those things, Charles has indicated, might require him to enter the political arena. The former basketball star has repeatedly said he is contemplating a run for governor of Alabama. That is the state where Charles was born and spent his childhood and youth.

CHAPTER TWO

"THE ROUND MOUND OF REBOUND"

Charles Wade Barkley was born on February 20, 1963, in the rural town of Leeds, Alabama. He weighed about six pounds at birth. Charles was a sickly infant who suffered from anemia. This condition is characterized by a lack of energy. It is caused by an inadequate quantity of red blood cells. When Charles was six weeks old, doctors decided that he needed a blood transfusion. Eventually his health improved.

Charles's parents, Frank Barkley and Charcey Glenn, divorced while Charles was still a baby. Frank Barkley moved away from Leeds. Charcey later remarried, but her new husband died in a car accident while Charles was in grade school. The boy would grow up without a father. It caused him a great deal of pain, he would later admit. "I hurt to the extent that I wish [my father] had been there and hurt that he wasn't," Charles told an interviewer. "I was very angry and very resentful."

Charles was raised by his mother and his grandmother, Johnnie Mae Edwards. The family was poor. Charcey cleaned homes for a living, while Johnnie Mae worked in a meat factory. Their hardworking example and their sacrifice, Charles would later say, strongly influenced him.

Big Dreams

As a kid, Charles was overweight. Still, he dreamed of a career in professional basketball. Early on, that didn't seem likely. In 10th grade, Charles tried out for Leeds High School's basketball team. He was cut. But he refused to give up. He practiced constantly and confidently declared that he would one day be a star in the NBA.

Charles's hard work had begun to pay off by his junior year at Leeds High, when he made the varsity basketball squad. Still, he mostly rode the bench.

Over the summer before his senior year, Charles had a growth spurt. He shot up from 5'10" to 6'4". Charles was still hefty, weighing in at 240 pounds, but he was extraordinarily quick. As a starter for Leeds, he averaged 19 points and almost

Above: Charles Barkley's 1981 high school yearbook photo. Left: Charles (back row, third from left) with members of the Leeds High varsity basketball team.

18 rebounds per game, leading his team to a 26–3 record and a berth in the Alabama state championships.

Despite his fine play, Charles went virtually unnoticed by college scouts. Going into the state basketball tournament, Charles had just one scholarship offer, from a community college in Boaz, Alabama. That was about to change.

When Leeds advanced to the semifinals of the Alabama state basketball tournament, it faced Huntsville's S. R. Butler High. Butler featured Bobby Lee Hurt, a 6'9" McDonald's All-American. In 1981, Hurt was considered the top high school recruit in the state of Alabama. An assistant coach from Auburn University was at the semifinal game to see Hurt play. He came away amazed—not by the play of Bobby Lee Hurt but by the play of Charles Barkley. Charles lit up Hurt for 26 points. The assistant coach excitedly telephoned Auburn head coach Sonny Smith with the news that he'd just seen "a fat guy . . . who can play like the wind."

Smith quickly called Charles Barkley and offered him a scholarship. Charles accepted the offer. His hard work had paid off.

College Standout

In the fall of 1981, Charles Barkley entered Auburn University in Auburn, Alabama. The shy, overweight freshman was a business administration major.

When the basketball season began, Charles quickly won the hearts of Auburn fans. He blocked shots, he grabbed rebounds, he sometimes dribbled the length of the floor and threw down thunderous dunks. His weight sometimes ballooned above 300 pounds, but this didn't seem to slow him down on the court. Playing center against taller players, Charles led the Southeastern Conference (SEC) in rebounding for three straight seasons. This, combined with his massive

Auburn's Charles Barkley goes airborne as Vanderbilt University's Bobby Westbrooks tries to defend him, February 13, 1984.

girth, earned him the nickname "the Round Mound of Rebound."

Over the course of his college career, Charles shot better than 68 percent from the field, averaging over 14 points per game. He also averaged 9.6 rebounds per game. Charles was named the SEC Player of the Year for the 1983–84 season, his junior year. Years later, he would be named SEC Player of the Decade for the 1980s.

Despite the heroics of "the Round Mound of Rebound," Auburn's teams were mediocre. Auburn's lone appearance in the NCAA men's basketball tournament during Charles's time at the university came in 1984. In the first round, Auburn faced Richmond. Charles turned in an outstanding performance, scoring 23 points and pulling down 17 rebounds. Nevertheless, Auburn lost in a heartbreaker, 72–71.

To the NBA

Charles decided to skip his senior year at Auburn and enter the NBA draft. He didn't imagine that he'd have a Hall of Fame career. Rather, he simply wanted to earn enough money to help his family live comfortably. "I knew I had a God-given ability to rebound," Charles would recall. "But I never averaged more than 14 points a game in college. So I was just hoping I could score 10 points and get 10 rebounds a game for a few years and make some money to take care of my family."

On the eve of the draft, many NBA general managers had concerns about Charles Barkley. First, they wondered whether

READ MORE

The 1984 NBA draft class, one of the best in history, included four players who would appear on the league's list of 50 greatest players of all time. Turn to page 46 to find out who they are.

The Philadelphia 76ers' first-round draft pick is introduced to fans and the media at a June 19, 1984, press conference.

he'd be able to control his weight. Second, there were questions about his work ethic. Stories abounded that Charles had chafed under the strict discipline of Auburn's Sonny Smith.

The Philadelphia 76ers decided to take a chance on Charles Barkley. The Sixers took Charles in the first round, with the fifth overall pick. Born and raised in rural Alabama, Charles was about to find out what life was like in a big city in the East.

CHAPTER THREE

SIR CHARLES OF THE PHILADELPHIA 76ers

In the summer of 1984, Charles Barkley reported to the Philadelphia 76ers' training camp weighing about 300 pounds. "He's so fat his bathtub has stretch marks," declared Sixers general manager Pat Williams.

Nevertheless, Williams, head coach Billy Cunningham, and the rest of the 76ers organization were prepared to exercise some patience with Charles Barkley. They believed that the rookie could play a key role on the team.

Charles was signed to a four-year, $2 million contract. He would be able to take care of his mother and grandmother after all. Charles soon bought them a five-bedroom house in Leeds.

Big-Impact Rookie

The 76ers team that Charles Barkley joined in 1984 was a talented group. It featured two legends—forward Julius "Dr. J" Erving and center Moses Malone—in addition to forward Bobby Jones, one of the NBA's best defenders; Maurice Cheeks, an outstanding point guard; and streaky shooting guard Andrew Toney. Paced by these players, the 76ers had won an NBA championship in 1983, sweeping the Los Angeles Lakers in the Finals.

But the team was aging. Erving was in his 13th year as a pro, Malone and Jones in their 10th seasons. Sixers officials hoped Charles Barkley would be able to provide a spark when these front-court stars needed a rest.

When he arrived in Philadelphia, Charles was a quiet and reserved 21-year-old. He often addressed reporters as "sir,"

Rookie Charles Barkley rumbles toward the hoop ahead of the Milwaukee Bucks' Terry Cummings. Charles averaged 14 points per game in his first pro season.

something Philadelphia sportswriters were certainly not used to. Charles was also in awe of Julius Erving, but the Doctor put him at ease. "I remember being so damn nervous before my first day of camp in 1984," Charles recalled.

> I had called and asked my friends, "What do you think I should call Julius Erving? Do I just call him 'Doc' or 'Dr. J' or 'Mr. Erving?'" I was really nervous about it because . . . this man was what you aspired to be, as a professional athlete and a man. At the start of the first practice he came over and said, "Hey, I'm Julius," and I breathed a sigh of relief. I'm lucky to have started my career in Philadelphia where I could be influenced by him.

Charles was also influenced by Moses Malone. Early in his career, some Sixers teammates accused Charles of laziness. Malone gave the young player a piece of advice that he took to heart. "You can come in here every day and work your [butt] off and still not make it," the veteran center told Charles. "But I can guarantee you if you come in here and don't work you won't make it.'"

Under the tutelage of Julius Erving and Moses Malone, Charles Barkley adjusted to the NBA. He quickly won

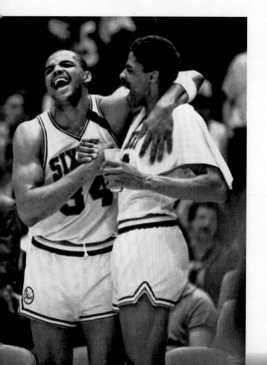

Charles celebrates a Sixers victory with Julius Erving. "I'm lucky to have started my career in Philadelphia where I could be influenced by him," Charles would later write of the legendary Dr. J.

over Philadelphia fans with his fearless, all-out style of play. In one game during his rookie season, Charles unleashed a dunk that was so forceful it moved the basket support, which weighed more than a ton, a full six inches. NBA big men soon learned that if they stood between Charles Barkley and a rebound, they'd better brace themselves for contact. Kareem Abdul-Jabbar, the great Los Angeles Lakers center, was asked whether he'd ever seen a player crash into other bodies with such abandon. "Earl Campbell and Jim Brown," Abdul-Jabbar replied, citing two bruising NFL running backs. "Nobody in this sport."

Charles Barkley's commanding presence on the floor earned him a new nickname to replace "the Round Mound of Rebound." Fans now began calling him "Sir Charles." Statistically, Sir Charles turned in a solid rookie season. He played in all 82 of the 76ers' regular-season games, averaging more than 28 minutes per game. His scoring average of 14 points per game was fourth on the team, and his 8.6 rebounds per game ranked second. Charles's fine play was recognized with a spot on the NBA's All-Rookie First Team.

Charles continued to play well in the postseason. He averaged nearly 15 points and more than 11 rebounds per game in the playoffs. The 76ers advanced to the Eastern Conference Finals before being stopped by the Boston Celtics. Unfortunately, this would be the best playoff showing during Charles's eight-year tenure in Philadelphia.

Continuing to Improve

In 1985–86, Charles built on the success of his excellent rookie season. He averaged 20 points per game. His 12.8 rebounds per game ranked second in the NBA. Charles was named to the All-NBA Second Team. Although the 76ers posted a regular-season record of 54–28, fourth best in the NBA, they fell to the Milwaukee Bucks in the Eastern Conference Semifinals. Charles's play during the series was outstanding: he grabbed nearly 16 rebounds and scored 25 points per game.

At the start of his third NBA season, the 23-year-old Charles Barkley began to emerge as a leader of the 76ers. Julius Erving was starting his farewell season with the team, and veteran center Moses Malone had been traded to Washington. During the 1986–87 season, Sir Charles dropped 23 points per game and grabbed a league-best 14.6 rebounds per game. For the second consecutive year, he was named to the All-NBA Second Team. After the retirement of Julius Erving at season's end, Charles was named the 76ers' team co-captain.

Sounding Off

If Charles Barkley had established himself as one of the NBA's young stars, the once-shy kid from Alabama had also acquired a reputation for making controversial statements. Charles said

Charles joined Sixers teammates Julius Erving and Maurice Cheeks on the 1987 Eastern Conference All-Star Game roster. For Charles it was the first of 11 All-Star appearances.

what was on his mind, and not everyone liked this. Often, after the 76ers lost a game, Charles sounded off about his team's lack of hustle, lack of talent, or lack of heart. It should be noted that Charles didn't spare himself after a bad performance, but some teammates and club officials didn't appreciate being called out in the press.

Charles believed he was labeled a troublemaker not simply because he was outspoken and controversial but also because he is black. "I would be asked a question after a loss or in the middle of a bad stretch about the 76ers' chances of seriously contending that year or making a run in the playoffs," Charles recalled in his memoir *I May Be Wrong but I Doubt It*.

> And I would say, "Our team isn't good enough," or, "We've got to get better in certain areas if we're going to compete at the championship level." I guess I could have tiptoed around it and given some vanilla answer, but that's not me. And besides, . . . I was assessing the situation as I saw it. The headlines the next day would say, "BARKLEY BLASTS TEAMMATES!"

Charles believed that when white professional athletes made similar comments in similar situations, the reaction was different. The media, he said, "perceive that the white player is a team guy only concerned with team goals when he speaks up about what the team needs, but they perceive that the black player when he speaks up about the team's needs is a malcontent."

Success on the Court, Troubles off the Court

If controversy seemed to follow him, Charles always appeared able to put distractions out of his mind when he stepped onto the basketball court. In 1987–88, his fourth season in the league, Charles averaged a career-best 28.3 points per game. He also pulled down 11.9 rebounds per game. He was named to the All-NBA First Team for the first time. The 76ers, however, failed to make the playoffs for the first time in Charles's young career.

Charles led the Sixers back to the playoffs the following year. His 25.8 points and 12.5 rebounds per game were both team bests. Now recognized as one of the top players in the league, Charles was again named to the All-Star Team and the All-NBA First Team. But the superstar couldn't save his team from being swept by the New York Knicks in the first round of the playoffs.

In the middle of the season, on February 9, 1989, Charles had married Maureen Blumhardt, his longtime girlfriend. Later in the year, the couple welcomed a daughter, Christiana.

During his next two seasons, Charles played at the high level basketball fans had come to expect of him. In 1989–90, he made the All-NBA First Team for the third straight year, and he finished second in the MVP voting to Magic Johnson of the Los Angeles Lakers. In 1990–91, Charles again received All-NBA First Team honors. He was also named MVP of the All-Star Game, scoring 17 points and grabbing 22 rebounds to lead

READ MORE

Michael Jordan led the Chicago Bulls to NBA dominance during the 1990s. Turn to page 48 to find out more.

his East squad to a 116–114 victory over the West. Yet Charles's playoff frustrations continued. The Sixers' 1989–90 and 1990–91 campaigns both ended with four-games-to-one losses in the Eastern Conference Semifinals to Michael Jordan's Chicago Bulls.

Even as he continued to shine as a basketball player, Charles Barkley was generating more controversy with his behavior. In

March of 1991, during a game against the New Jersey Nets at the Meadowlands Arena, Charles was heckled by a fan who repeatedly shouted racial epithets at him. Charles grew so angry that he spit at the heckler. He missed, however, and the spit landed on a 10-year-old girl named Lauren Rose. Embarrassed and ashamed, Charles apologized for the incident, and he eventually developed a long-standing friendship with the young girl and her family. Still, the ugly incident outraged fans and nonfans alike.

Charles's image was further tarnished in December of 1991, when he was arrested in Milwaukee for allegedly breaking a man's nose during a fight. Charles was ultimately acquitted of any crime. The following year, Charles was arrested alongside teammate Jayson Williams after a barroom brawl in Chicago. But those charges were eventually dropped, too. According to Charles, he never looked for trouble. But neither did he avoid going out in public just to avoid potential confrontations with people who might want to pick a fight with someone famous.

Time to Move On

On the court, Charles's eighth and final season with the Philadelphia 76ers was a disaster. Though his numbers were still great—23.1 points and 11.1 rebounds per game—the team finished last in the Atlantic Division with a 35–47 record. Angry and disappointed about

This mug shot of Charles Barkley was taken in 1997, following an altercation Charles had with another man at an Orlando, Florida, club. Charles's brushes with the law began during his early years with the 76ers.

missing the playoffs again, Charles made it clear that he wanted to play for a team that had a better chance of winning a championship.

On June 17, 1992, the Philadelphia 76ers traded Charles Barkley to the Phoenix Suns for Tim Perry, Andrew Lang, and Jeff Hornacek. Charles had gotten his wish. At a news conference to announce the trade, Sixers general manager Jim Lynam said, "Charles has said he wants to be on a contender, and in all honesty, if we had kept Charles, I'm not sure we could strike that posture. We had to make changes."

CHAPTER FOUR

A NEW BEGINNING

After eight seasons with the Philadelphia 76ers, Charles Barkley was moving to a new team. Before he joined the Phoenix Suns, however, Charles helped lead the U.S. men's Olympic basketball team to a gold medal in Barcelona, Spain, in the summer of 1992. But Charles had his eyes focused on another goal—an NBA championship.

The Phoenix Suns team that Charles joined was a good one. The Suns had posted four consecutive 50-win seasons. But each year, they had faltered in the playoffs. Club officials hoped that Charles Barkley could get the team to the top.

The Suns were a juggernaut during the 1992–93 regular season. Their 62–20 record was best in the NBA. Charles led the way with 25.6 points and 12.2 rebounds per game. He was voted the league's MVP.

READ MORE

The U.S. men's basketball team that won a gold medal at the 1992 Summer Olympics in Barcelona, Spain, is widely regarded as the greatest collection of basketball talent ever assembled. Turn to page 49 to learn more about the Dream Team.

Phoenix continued to roll during the postseason. The Suns dispatched the Los Angeles Lakers in the first round of the playoffs,

New uniform, familiar sight: Sir Charles dribbles in the open court during the 1992–93 season. Charles won league MVP honors in his first season with the Phoenix Suns.

then rolled over the San Antonio Spurs in the Western Conference Semifinals. The Western Conference Finals was a grueling seven-game series, but ultimately Charles's 26.6 points and 13.6 rebounds per game paced the Suns to victory over the Seattle Supersonics.

Awaiting Charles and his teammates in the NBA Finals were the Chicago Bulls. Chicago had won the previous two NBA championships.

The series was a memorable one. Chicago took the first two games, on Phoenix's home court, despite Charles Barkley's 42-point outburst in Game 2. In Game 3, Phoenix battled back to win a triple-overtime thriller in Chicago, 129–121. Michael Jordan proved too much for the Suns in Game 4, scoring 55 points to lead the Bulls to a 111–105 win. In Game 5, the Suns staved off elimination with a 10-point victory. They headed back to Phoenix needing to win both remaining games. Instead, the Bulls eked out a 99–98 Game 6 victory to clinch their third straight championship.

In some respects, 1992–93 marked the high-water mark of Charles Barkley's NBA career. Charles won his only MVP Award and reached his only Finals. He was now 30 years old, and injuries plagued him constantly. One injury almost forced him to retire the following season.

"I Am Not a Role Model"

If his career was on the wane, Charles was still just as capable as ever of stirring up controversy. In 1993, he appeared in an advertisement for Nike whose theme was "I am not a role model." In the ad, Charles said that kids shouldn't look up to athletes but rather to their parents and other adults they knew well. The ad was very poorly received, and Charles was lambasted in the media.

Surrounded by San Antonio Spurs, Charles puts in a layup during Game 3 of the Western Conference Semifinals, May 15, 1993. Phoenix won the series, four games to two, then defeated the Seattle Supersonics to earn a trip to the NBA Finals.

Charles stood by the ad's message, however. "Remember, the main theme was 'I am not a role model.' And for that, I got ripped," Charles noted. "How crazy is it to get slammed for saying, 'Listen to your parents, listen to your teachers, listen to the responsible adults in your neighborhood or people who have done something with their lives.'"

Aches and Pains

During the 1993–94 season, his second with the Suns, Charles started to have repeated difficulties with his back. The pain was so bad that he said he would retire after the season. Despite the pain, however, he played on, leading his team to the Western Conference Semifinals, where they lost in seven games. Shortly after the playoffs, Charles announced that he had decided to fight through the pain and continue to play.

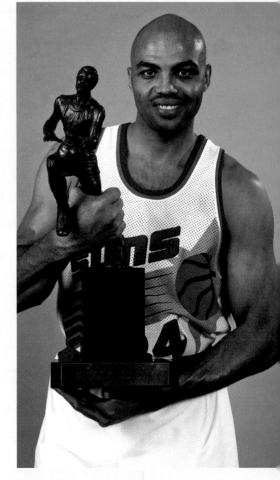

Charles poses with the Maurice Podoloff Trophy, given to the NBA's Most Valuable Player, 1993.

Then, during the summer of 1994, people started to ask questions about Charles's dedication to basketball and about his work ethic. A story in the *Phoenix Gazette* reported that Charles had discontinued a planned eight-week rehabilitation program for his back after just four days. Worse, he had gone to Philadelphia to golf.

Charles began the 1994–95 season on the injured list. He ultimately appeared in 65 regular-season games, and he played effectively. Charles averaged 23 points and 11.1 rebounds per game. In the playoffs, however, the Suns were bounced in the Western Conference Semifinals for the second consecutive year by the Houston Rockets. Charles was bothered by a leg injury throughout the seven-game series.

In 1995–96, the Suns fell to a mediocre 41–41 regular-season record. They lost in the first round of the playoffs. During the season, Charles very publicly stated that he wanted to be traded to a team capable of winning an NBA championship. Charles threatened to retire if he wasn't traded. The sun had set on his time in Phoenix.

One Last Chance

During the summer of 1996, Charles Barkley was traded to the Houston Rockets for Sam Cassell, Robert Horry, Mark Bryant, and Chucky Brown. In Houston, Charles joined NBA legends Hakeem Olajuwon and Clyde Drexler. He felt that this would be his final chance to win the elusive NBA championship. "I'm very excited," he said after the trade. "Obviously, it's something I wanted to do. Houston was my first priority."

Charles wanted to win a championship more than anything, but Drexler and Olajuwon were also nearing the end of their careers. In their first season together, the trio made it all the way to the Western Conference Finals, but lost to the Utah Jazz in six games. For his part, Charles averaged more than 19 points and 13.5 rebounds per game. But he missed almost 30 games because of injuries.

READ MORE

Winning an NBA championship is the dream of every basketball player. But because basketball is a team sport, some of the most talented superstars never taste a title. See page 50 to find out about some of the best players never to win a championship.

Clyde Drexler laughs at a comment by his new teammate during a press conference introducing Charles Barkley to the Houston media, August 19, 1996. Phoenix had traded Charles to the Houston Rockets for four players.

In the next season, the Rockets managed only a 41–41 record, and the team lost to the Utah Jazz in the first round of the playoffs. To make matters worse, Clyde Drexler retired at season's end.

Before the 1998–99 season, Charles Barkley saw one last chance at winning a championship when the team signed another aging superstar, Scottie Pippen. Pippen had won six titles playing alongside Michael Jordan in Chicago. But the duo of Barkley and Pippen never clicked, and the Rockets lost in the first round of the playoffs once again.

Following the season, Pippen and Charles said very negative things about each other to members of the media. Pippen was traded to the Portland Trailblazers. Soon after, Charles announced that the 1999–2000 season would be his last.

"I'm getting out at the right time for two reasons," Charles told a group of reporters in the early weeks of his final season.

> No. 1, the game has changed, the players have changed. No. 2, I'm not good enough to do anything about it anymore. Three, four or five years ago, if you had a lot of knuckleheads on your team, you didn't need help. You still could go out there and pretty much win the game by yourself. Now, I can't do that anymore. I'm not frustrated at other people. I'm frustrated at myself because I can't play like other people.

Doing It His Way

On December 8, 1999, the Houston Rockets were in Philadelphia, where Charles had begun his pro career and where he remained very popular. Sixers fans gave him numerous standing ovations. It was to be a night of celebration. It turned into something else.

With 4:09 left in the first quarter, Charles went up to block a shot by Sixers forward Tyrone Hill. He fell, hitting the floor hard. Charles said he knew immediately that this was the end of his career. He had ruptured a tendon in his left knee.

"I guess the big fella in the sky wanted me to finish right where I started," Charles told reporters after the game. "There

End of a career: Charles Barkley crashes to the floor with a serious knee injury during a game against the 76ers, December 8, 1999.

were a lot of people here tonight who saw me play my first game and saw me play my last game."

As it turned out, this wouldn't quite be Charles's last game. On April 19, 2000, with the Houston Rockets hosting the Vancouver Grizzlies, Charles played for a few minutes and picked up two points. He also addressed fans and teammates,

A legend says good-bye: Charles Barkley thanks teammates and fans after his final NBA game, April 19, 2000.

thanking them for a great 16 years. Then he walked off the court for the last time.

Before the game, Charles had told a reporter from Houston, "I owe everything in my life to basketball. I mean you think about it. I'm rich beyond my wildest expectations, I've got luxuries, I've met kids, I've met kings, I've met queens, I've met presidents and I'm 37. . . . I owe everything in my life to basketball."

Though Charles Barkley's career as an NBA player had come to an end, he would not remain out of the spotlight for long.

CHAPTER FIVE

LIFE AFTER BASKETBALL

On April 19, 2000, just hours before suiting up to play in his final game, Charles Barkley sat down with a reporter from the Houston Rockets' Web site for an exclusive interview. The first question the reporter asked had nothing to do with the game, his injury, how he was feeling emotionally, or even with the sport of basketball. Instead, the reporter asked, "Will it be a natural progression for you to become a member of the media?" Charles had become so comfortable in the spotlight that the reporter's question was a natural one.

The Sports Analyst

In 2001, Charles Barkley joined announcer Ernie Johnson and former NBA player Kenny "the Jet" Smith as an in-studio analyst for *Inside the NBA*, the TNT network's weekly coverage of the league. As a broadcaster, Charles was an instant success. Viewers loved his flamboyant style and outrageous comments. Said Fritz Quindt of *The Sporting News*, "Now a rookie-of-the-year analyst on Turner Sports' 'Inside the NBA,' his role is the same as it ever was; he's on TV a couple of times a week, shooting from the hip, ever the go-to guy." During his first year with the show, *Inside the NBA* received an Emmy Award.

Basketball legend Magic Johnson (left) shares a laugh with *Inside the NBA* hosts Ernie Johnson, Kenny Smith, and Charles Barkley, 2004. Charles's winning personality made him a natural for the show.

As always, Sir Charles could be loved or hated, but it was impossible to ignore him. In 2002, TNT gave Charles and his partners a weekly Thursday night show, called *Listen Up! Charles Barkley with Ernie Johnson and Kenny Smith*. That same year, *Sports Illustrated* named Charles its "Personality of the Year." The CNN cable network regularly featured Charles as a guest on its show *Talkback Live*. Charles even announced an occasional baseball game.

By 2008, Charles had eight strong years as a broadcaster behind him. In February of that year, he signed a multiyear contract extension with TNT.

The Writer

During his playing career, Charles Barkley cowrote two books. *Outrageous! The Fine Life and Flagrant Good Times of Basketball's*

Irresistible Force, with Roy S. Johnson, was released in 1992. *Sir Charles: The Wit and Wisdom of Charles Barkley*, with Rick Reilly, followed in 1995.

After his retirement from basketball, Charles collaborated with *Washington Post* sportswriter Michael Wilbon on two more books. In the first, 2003's *I May Be Wrong but I Doubt It*, Charles shared his views on politics, race, the media, former players, and much more.

In 2005, Barkley and Wilbon's *Who's Afraid of a Large Black Man?* was published. This was unlike anything Charles had done before. Racism, which Charles describes as "the biggest cancer of my lifetime," is the book's central theme, and the format is unique. Charles sat down with a dozen important public figures, from Tiger Woods to Bill Clinton to George Lopez, and had candid conversations about race. Like *I May Be Wrong but I Doubt It*, the book was a huge success.

The Philanthropist

Charles Barkley donated a great deal of money to a variety of charitable causes long before his retirement. After he retired, however, people really began paying attention to his good deeds. Charles has made so many contributions over the years that it's impossible to catalog them all. Among the largest recipients of his donations are groups in his native Alabama, including the Auburn University Foundation, the Cornerstone Schools in Alabama, and Leeds High School. Charles has also made numerous donations to a variety of children's organizations through the Charles Barkley Foundation, a nonprofit group he founded.

The Politician?

Long before his retirement, Charles Barkley talked—sometimes seriously, sometimes not—about going into politics. He toyed

The author with his 2005 book. For *Who's Afraid of a Large Black Man?*, Charles conducted a dozen interviews with prominent Americans—including former president Bill Clinton, civil rights leader Jesse Jackson, golfer Tiger Woods, and actor Morgan Freeman—and elicited their thoughts about the subject of race.

Charles poses with children during the opening of the Charles Barkley Reading and Learning Center at the Boys & Girls Club of Peoria, Arizona, October 1, 2004. Charles is a big supporter of programs for children.

with the idea of running for governor of Alabama in 1995. Nothing came of that talk.

In the summer of 2006, however, Charles again brought up the possibility of running for political office. While addressing a convention of public school board members in Destin, Florida, Charles said, "Alabama, that's my home. I'm thinking about running for governor; they need my help."

In October 2008, in an interview with Campbell Brown of CNN, Charles said that he did in fact plan to run for governor of Alabama in 2014, and that his priority would be improving public education in the state. Many political observers believe Charles would be a formidable candidate in Alabama. "He's definitely going to be taken seriously," declared former governor Don Siegelman.

READ MORE

A handful of American professional athletes have made the transition from sports to politics. Find out about some of them on page 51.

Charles claims he feels a call to serve. "I really believe I was put on Earth to do more than play basketball and stockpile money," he once said. "I really want to help people improve their lives, and what's left is for me to decide how best to do that." Perhaps, after all, Charles Barkley is a role model.

The ever-popular Sir Charles at an event during the NBA's 2008 All-Star Weekend, February 15.

CROSS-CURRENTS

The 50 Greatest Players of All Time

On June 6, 1946, the Basketball Association of America (BAA) was formed in New York City. The BAA would change its name to the National Basketball Association three years later, following a merger with a smaller pro basketball league.

In 1996, to mark its 50th year, the NBA put together a list of its 50 greatest players of all time. The list was compiled by a panel of former players and coaches, current and former general managers and team executives, and basketball writers and broadcasters. The former players weren't allowed to vote for themselves.

NBA commissioner David Stern unveiled the list in New York City on October 29, 1996. No attempt was made to rank the players within the list. Players' names appeared alphabetically.

Wilt Chamberlain shoots a jumper over Bill Russell. Both big men were selected for the NBA's list of the 50 greatest players of all time.

"The List"

Kareem Abdul-Jabbar	Karl Malone
Nate Archibald	Moses Malone
Paul Arizin	Pete Maravich
Charles Barkley	Kevin McHale
Rick Barry	George Mikan
Elgin Baylor	Earl Monroe
Dave Bing	Hakeem Olajuwon
Larry Bird	Shaquille O'Neal
Wilt Chamberlain	Robert Parish
Bob Cousy	Bob Pettit
Dave Cowens	Scottie Pippen
Billy Cunningham	Willis Reed
Dave DeBusschere	Oscar Robertson
Clyde Drexler	David Robinson
Julius Erving	Bill Russell
Patrick Ewing	Dolph Schayes
Walt Frazier	Bill Sharman
George Gervin	John Stockton
Hal Greer	Isiah Thomas
John Havlicek	Nate Thurmond
Elvin Hayes	Wes Unseld
Magic Johnson	Bill Walton
Sam Jones	Jerry West
Michael Jordan	Lenny Wilkens
Jerry Lucas	James Worthy

The Class of 1984

Each year in June, NBA coaches, general managers, and club executives gather for the league's draft. The ranks of graduating college players and others eligible for the draft always include a number of excellent prospects. But there are no guarantees that a promising draft pick will ever make it in the NBA.

The 1984 draft class contained some very highly touted college players. And, as it turned out, a number of players drafted that year would go on to have Hall of Fame pro careers. Four, in fact, would be picked for the NBA's list of 50 greatest players of all time.

The Houston Rockets had the first overall pick in the 1984 draft, and they chose Hakeem Olajuwon. The Nigerian-born big man, who had attended the University of Houston, would spend 17 of his 18 pro seasons with Houston. Olajuwon averaged 21.8 points and 11.1 rebounds per game. He also established the NBA career record for blocked shots, with 3,830. Olajuwon led Houston to back-to-back titles in 1984 and 1985, and he won Finals MVP honors both years.

Portland had the second pick in the 1984 draft, and Trailblazers

Michael Jordan slams home a dunk during the 1998 NBA Finals. MJ spoiled the championship dreams of many NBA stars while helping to bring six titles to Chicago.

fans would come to regret the decision club officials made. Portland selected the University of Kentucky's Sam Bowie. Bowie, a 7'1" center/forward, had a lackluster, injury-plagued 10-year pro career.

The Chicago Bulls benefited from Portland's misguided selection. With the third pick in the 1984 draft, Chicago selected the University of North Carolina's Michael Jordan. Jordan merely went on to become perhaps the best player in NBA history. He won five league MVP awards; led Chicago to six championships, garnering six Finals MVP awards; and finished his 15-year career with a 30.1 points-per-game scoring average, tied with Wilt Chamberlain for highest ever.

Like Portland, the Dallas Mavericks could have chosen better. With the fourth pick the Mavs selected University of North Carolina big man Sam Perkins, who averaged a modest 11.9 points per game over a 17-year pro career. With the next pick in the draft, the Philadelphia 76ers got Charles Barkley.

The Utah Jazz unquestionably made the best sleeper pick in the 1984 draft. With the 16th overall pick, Utah chose a 6'1" guard from Gonzaga University. In 19 seasons with the Jazz, John Stockton was the model of a successful, consistent point guard. He established career records for assists (15,806) and steals (3,265).

Stockton, Olajuwan, Jordan, and Barkley—all members of the draft class of 1984—were selected for the NBA's list of 50 greatest players of all time.

Dominating the 1990s

Many of the great NBA players of the 1990s never got a championship ring. That is largely because of one man: Michael Jordan. Widely considered the best basketball player ever, Jordan dominated the NBA during the 1990s. A five-time league MVP, he also won six Finals MVP awards, leading his Chicago Bulls teams to NBA championships in 1991, 1992, 1993, 1996, 1997, and 1998.

As great a player as Jordan was, however, he couldn't have won six titles without a strong supporting cast. In various seasons, Jordan's teammates included offensive-minded forward Scottie Pippen; Dennis Rodman, a defensive specialist who was among the best rebounders in the league; point guards John Paxson and Steve Kerr; forward Toni Kukoc, a dangerous scorer; and big man Horace Grant. The Bulls were coached masterfully by Phil Jackson. In addition to his six championships with Chicago, the redoubtable Jackson would win three straight titles at the helm of the Los Angeles Lakers (2000, 2001, and 2002).

The Original Dream Team

Many considered it to be the greatest team ever assembled in any sport. The 1992 U.S. men's Olympic basketball team consisted of 11 of the best NBA players and Christian Laettner, college basketball's brightest star. All-Stars Michael Jordan, Earvin "Magic" Johnson, Larry Bird, Charles Barkley, Clyde Drexler, David Robinson, Patrick Ewing, Scottie Pippen, Karl Malone, John Stockton, and Chris Mullin, along with Laettner, blew away the competition in Barcelona, Spain. The Dream Team beat its opponents by an astounding average of 44 points per game and took home the gold medal.

Before 1992, NBA players had not been allowed to compete in the Olympic Games. By the time of the Barcelona Olympics, the international popularity of basketball and the NBA had exploded. The members of the Dream Team enjoyed rock-star status, and their celebrity eclipsed all the other great athletes who competed at Barcelona. "It was like Elvis and the Beatles put together," head coach Chuck Daly said of the experience.

The Dream Team poses for a portrait, Barcelona, Spain, July 25, 1992.

CROSS-CURRENTS

Best NBA Players Who Never Won a Championship

Pro athletes are judged not only by their individual accomplishments but also by how many championships they have won. Some of the NBA's best players never played on a championship team. These players include:

- **Patrick Ewing.** Ewing was the first overall pick in the 1985 NBA draft. He played 17 seasons, 15 of them for the New York Knicks. Over the course of his career, he averaged more than 20 points and nearly 10 rebounds per game. Although his New York Knicks reached the NBA Finals in 1994 and 1999, the team was never able to win it all. Patrick Ewing retired without a title to his name.

- **Karl Malone and John Stockton.** Malone, a 6'9" power forward, and Stockton, a 6'1" point guard, played together on the Utah Jazz from 1985 to 2003. In 1996, both men appeared on the NBA's list of 50 greatest players of all time. Stockton and Malone played in the NBA Finals in 1997 and 1998, but each time their Jazz team was stopped by the Chicago Bulls.

- **Charles Barkley.** The illustrious 16-year career of Sir Charles included almost every individual honor. But Charles's stints with Philadelphia, Phoenix, and Houston all ended without a championship ring.

From Athletics
to Politics

The sports arena and the political arena could hardly be more different. In the former, physical skills are paramount; in the latter, interpersonal skills and a command of policy are the keys to success. But in the United States pro athletes are celebrities, and name recognition is an advantage for politicians. Several sports stars have capitalized on their athletic success to enter politics.

One high-profile athlete who successfully made the transition from sports to politics is Jack Kemp. Kemp, a star quarterback in the American Football League, led his Buffalo Bills to back-to-back AFL championships and in 1965 was named the league's MVP. After his retirement from football, Kemp became a leading figure in the Republican Party. He served nine terms in the U.S. Congress, representing a district in western New York. He later ran unsuccessfully for president and vice president of the United States.

Basketball Hall of Famer Bill Bradley, a guard/forward for the New York Knicks, played on two NBA championship teams during his 10-year pro career. In 1978, one year after retiring from basketball, Bradley won election to the U.S. Senate. He represented New Jersey for three terms. In 2000, Bradley ran for the Democratic Party's presidential nomination. He lost to Vice President Al Gore.

In 1964, pitcher Jim Bunning hurled a perfect game for the Philadelphia Phillies. The right-hander, a nine-time All-Star, was inducted into the National Baseball Hall of Fame in 1996. Bunning, a Kentuckian, served 12 years in the U.S. House of Representatives before winning election to the Senate in 1998. He was reelected in 2004.

Chronology

1963: Charles Wade Barkley is born on February 20 in Leeds, Alabama.

1981: Begins his college career at Auburn University.

1984: Is selected by the Philadelphia 76ers as the fifth overall pick in the NBA draft.

1987: Plays in his first NBA All-Star Game.

1989: Marries Maureen Blumhardt on February 9.

1991: Spits on fan Lauren Rose in a March game at the Meadowlands in New Jersey.

1992: Is traded to the Phoenix Suns on June 17. Wins a gold medal at the Olympics in Barcelona, Spain, as a member of the "Dream Team."

1993: Appears in the infamous "I am not a role model" commercial. Win league MVP honors.

1996: Is traded to the Houston Rockets for Sam Cassell, Mark Bryant, Robert Horry, and Chuck Atkins on August 19. Named one of the NBA's 50 greatest players of all time.

2000: Plays his final NBA game on April 19 against the Vancouver Grizzlies.

2002: After joining TNT as a broadcaster the previous year, is named "Personality of the Year" by *Sports Illustrated*.

2003: Publishes *I May Be Wrong but I Doubt It*.

2005: Releases the book *Who's Afraid of a Large Black Man?*

2006: Is elected to the Naismith Memorial Basketball Hall of Fame in April.

2008: Is sued by a Las Vegas casino for nonpayment of a $400,000 gambling debt, which he then settles. During an interview in October, announces his intention to run for governor of Alabama in 2014. In December, is arrested in Arizona for driving under the influence of alcohol.

Accomplishments/Awards

NBA All-Rookie First Team, 1985

All-NBA First Team, 1988, 1989, 1990, 1991, 1993

All-NBA Second Team, 1986, 1987, 1992, 1994, 1995

NBA All-Star, 1987–1997

NBA All-Star Game MVP, 1991

NBA MVP, 1993

Olympic Gold Medalist, 1992, 1996

Elected to Basketball Hall of Fame, 2006

CHARLES BARKLEY CAREER SEASON AVERAGES

Year	Team	G	GS	MPG	FG%	3P%	FT%	OFF	DEF	RPG	APG	SPG	BPG	TO	PF	PPG
84-85	PHI	82	60	28.6	0.545	0.167	0.733	3.20	5.30	8.60	1.9	1.16	0.98	2.55	3.70	14
85-86	PHI	80	80	36.9	0.572	0.227	0.685	4.40	8.40	12.80	3.9	2.16	1.56	4.38	4.20	20
86-87	PHI	68	62	40.3	0.594	0.202	0.761	5.70	8.90	14.60	4.9	1.75	1.53	4.74	3.70	23
87-88	PHI	80	80	39.6	0.587	0.28	0.751	4.80	7.10	11.90	3.2	1.25	1.29	3.8	3.50	28.3
88-89	PHI	79	79	39.1	0.579	0.216	0.753	5.10	7.40	12.50	4.1	1.59	0.85	3.22	3.30	25.8
89-90	PHI	79	79	39.1	0.6	0.217	0.749	4.60	6.90	11.50	3.9	1.87	0.63	3.08	3.20	25.2
90-91	PHI	67	67	37.3	0.57	0.284	0.722	3.90	6.30	10.10	4.2	1.64	0.49	3.13	2.60	27.6
91-92	PHI	75	75	38.4	0.552	0.234	0.695	3.60	7.50	11.10	4.1	1.81	0.59	3.13	2.60	23.1
92-93	PHO	76	76	37.6	0.52	0.305	0.765	3.10	9.10	12.20	5.1	1.57	0.97	3.07	2.60	25.6
93-94	PHO	65	65	35.4	0.495	0.27	0.704	3.00	8.10	11.20	4.6	1.55	0.57	3.17	2.50	21.6
94-95	PHO	68	66	35	0.486	0.338	0.748	3.00	8.10	11.10	4.1	1.62	0.66	2.21	3.00	23
95-96	PHO	71	71	37.1	0.5	0.28	0.777	3.40	8.10	11.60	3.7	1.61	0.79	3.07	2.90	23.2
96-97	HOU	53	53	37.9	0.484	0.283	0.694	4.00	9.50	13.50	4.7	1.3	0.47	2.85	2.90	19.2
97-98	HOU	68	41	33	0.485	0.214	0.746	3.50	8.10	11.70	3.20	1.04	0.41	2.16	2.80	15.20
98-99	HOU	42	40	36.3	0.478	0.16	0.719	4.00	8.30	12.30	4.60	1.02	0.31	2.38	2.10	16.10
99-00	HOU	20	18	31	0.477	0.231	0.645	3.60	6.90	10.50	3.20	0.70	0.20	2.20	2.40	14.50
CAREER	--	1,073	1,012	36.7	0.541	0.266	0.735	4.00	7.70	11.70	3.9	1.54	0.83	3.15	3.10	22.1
PLAYOFF	--	123	108	39.4	0.513	0.255	0.717	4.10	8.70	12.90	3.90	1.57	0.88	2.87	3.30	23.00
ALL-STAR	--	9	7	23.2	0.495	0.25	0.625	2.40	4.20	6.70	1.8	1.33	0.44	2.22	2.00	12.6

Further Reading

Barkley, Charles, with Rick Reilly. *Sir Charles: The Wit and Wisdom of Charles Barkley*. New York: Warner Books, 1998.

Barkley, Charles, with Roy S. Johnson. *Outrageous! The Fine Life and Flagrant Good Times of Basketball's Irresistible Force*. New York: Avon Books, 1993.

Barkley, Charles, with Michael Wilbon. *I May Be Wrong but I Doubt It*. New York: Random House, 2003.

___. *Who's Afraid of a Large Black Man?* New York: Penguin Press, 2005.

Internet Resources

http://www.nba.com/history/players/barkley_bio.html

> Charles Barkley's biography on the NBA's official Web site. Includes links to Charles's career statistics as well as pages of general NBA information.

http://search.espn.go.com/charles-barkley/

> ESPN's Charles Barkley page features stats and in-depth news stories about Charles.

http://search.sportsillustrated.cnn.com/pages/search.jsp?Coll=si_xml&QuerySubmit=true&Page=1&sites=si&query=charles+barkley

> Links to articles about Charles Barkley's life and career, from *Sports Illustrated*.

Publisher's Note: The Web sites listed on this page were active at the time of publication. The publisher is not responsible for Web sites that have changed their address or discontinued operation since the date of publication. The publisher reviews and updates the Web sites each time the book is reprinted.

Glossary

acquitted—declared innocent of a charge or crime.

candidate—a person who is being considered for a position, especially an elected office.

convention—an assembly or gathering of people for the purpose of addressing a specific issue.

elite—representing or belonging to the best in a particular field.

lambasted—harshly or severely criticized.

outspoken—frank; candid; tending to say things that others may be afraid to say.

philanthropist—a person who actively promotes the good of others (for example, by donating money to charitable causes).

pinnacle—the high point or best part of something.

tendon—an internal tissue that connects muscle to bone.

tutelage—guidance; instruction.

Chapter Notes

p. 8:   "He plays everything . . ." "Top 75 Greatest NBA Players of All Time," *SLAM*, March 2003. http://www.slam online.com

p. 11: "Basketball is really important . . ." David Aldridge, "Barkley Shares His Journey to the Hall of Fame," *Philadelphia Inquirer*, September 8, 2006.

p. 12: "I hurt to the extent . . ." Alan Richman, "Call Him 'Round Mound' at Your Peril; Charles Barkley's Bite Is Worse Than His Woof," *People* vol. 27, no. 17 (April 27, 1987). http://www.people.com/people/archive/article0,,20096148,00.html

p. 14: "a fat guy . . ." Michael Wilbon, "Barkley: the Great Wide Hope," *Washington Post*, April 23, 1984.

p. 16: "I knew I had . . ." Larry Platt, "Brilliant Careers: Charles Barkley," *Salon.com*, May 30, 2000. http://archive.salon.com/people/bc/2000/05/30/barkley/index.html

p. 18: "He's so fat . . ." Richman, "Call Him 'Round Mound.'"

p. 20: "I remember being . . ." Charles Barkley with Michael Wilbon, *I May Be Wrong but I Doubt It* (New York: Random House, 2003), 48.

p. 20: "You can come in here . . ." Ibid., 225.

p. 21: "Earl Campbell and . . ." Richman, "Call Him 'Round Mound.'"

p. 23: "I would be asked . . ." Barkley with Wilbon, I *May Be Wrong*, 48.

p. 23: "perceive that the white . . ." Ibid., 49.

p. 26: "Charles has said he wants . . ." Clifton Brown, "Bright Days for Suns: They Get Barkley," *New York Times*, June 18, 1992.

p. 31: Remember, the main theme . . ." Barkley with Wilbon, *I May Be Wrong*, 125.

p. 32: "I'm very excited . . ." "Barkley Confirms His Trade to Rockets," *New York Times*, August 19, 1996.

p. 34: "I'm getting out . . ." Mike Wise, "Barkley Is Getting a Harsh Reminder," *New York Times*, November 27, 1999.

p. 34: "I guess the big fella . . ." " Barkley's Career Ended by Knee Injury," *New York Times*, December 9, 1999.

p. 37: "I owe everything . . ." "Barkley One Last Time," April 19, 2000. http://www.nba.com/rockets/news/barkley_quotes000420.html

p. 38: "Will it be . . ." Ibid.

p. 38: "Now a rookie . . ." Fritz Quindt, "Viewers Hitching on to Chuckwagon—Television Broadcaster and Former Basketball Star Charles Barkley," *The Sporting News*, March 5, 2001.

p. 40: "the biggest cancer . . ." Charles Barkley, *Who's Afraid of a Large Black Man?*, edited by Michael Wilbon (New York, Penguin, 2005), ix.

p. 42: "Alabama, that's my home . . ." "Barkley Eyes Alabama Governor's Office as a Democrat," *USA Today*, July 27, 2006. http://www.usatoday.com/sports/basketball/2006-07-26-barkley-for-governor_x.htm

p. 43: "He's definitely going . . ." Ibid.

p. 43: "I really believe . . ." Brian M. Goodman, "Charles Barkley Eyes Run For Governor," *CBS News*, July 27, 2006. http://www.cbsnews.com/stories/2006/07/27/politics/main1842198.shtml

p. 49: "It was like Elvis . . ." "The Original Dream Team," *NBA.com*. http://www.nba.com/history/dreamT_moments.html

Index

Numbers in **bold italics** refer to captions.

Photo Credits

About the Author

JAMIE FEDORKO is the award-winning author of *The Intern Files: How to Get, Keep and Make the Most of Your Internship*. Born and raised in New York and an avid sports fan, Fedorko has worked with such publications as *GQ*, *Vibe*, *Paper*, and *Laptop* magazines as well as with CNBC Networks. This is his third book.